# ORNITHOGRAPHY

Also by Jessica Roux

*Floriography: An Illustrated Guide to the Victorian Language of Flowers*

Woodland Wardens: A 52-Card Oracle Deck & Guidebook

*The Wheel of the Year: An Illustrated Guide to Nature's Rhythms* (with Fiona Cook)

# ORNITHOGRAPHY

## An Illustrated Guide to Bird Lore & Symbolism

Jessica Roux

Andrews McMeel
PUBLISHING®

Andrews McMeel Publishing
a division of Andrews McMeel Universal
1130 Walnut Street, Kansas City, Missouri 64106

www.andrewsmcmeel.com

24 25 26 27 28 TEN 10 9 8 7 6 5 4 3 2 1

ISBN: 978-1-5248-8877-0

Library of Congress Control Number: 2024933731

Editor: Melissa Rhodes Zahorsky
Art Director: Diane Marsh
Production Editor: Elizabeth A. Garcia
Production Manager: Tamara Haus

ATTENTION: SCHOOLS AND BUSINESSES
Andrews McMeel books are available at quantity discounts with bulk purchase for educational, business, or sales promotional use. For information, please e-mail the Andrews McMeel Publishing Special Sales Department: sales@amuniversal.com.

# CONTENTS

For Nick

# INTRODUCTION

Birds have inspired us since the dawn of time: their elegance in flight, captivating songs, and delicate mannerisms spark hope and delight. For centuries, cultures around the world have looked to birds for meaning, often relying on these creatures to teach moral lessons, illuminate history, foretell victory, or warn of doom.

The divinatory observation of birds began long ago, at least as far back as ancient Greece, where ornithomancy—the interpretation of omens based on the movements and calls of birds—was integral to the culture. It paved the way for the ancient Roman practice of augury, from which we get the terms "auspicious," meaning a good omen, and "inauguration," a formal ceremony that, in Rome, would have involved looking to birds for signs from the gods. Augurs sought messages in how birds flew and at what height, the number of birds present, their songs, and even their eating patterns. The results of auguries were taken extremely seriously and heavily influenced Roman daily life, politics, and even military strategy.

While augury is no longer common practice, and we don't have a "language of birds" as standardized as the Victorian language of flowers, we can look to folklore, mythology, and history for insight into the symbolism associated with our feathered friends. By reflecting on dozens of such sources, I have assigned meanings to one hundred of my favorite birds, illustrating each one. While I've included many beloved species, like the robin, sparrow, and wren, I've found I am most fond of the "ugly ducklings": birds with peculiar proportions, curious colors, and fantastic feathers. Whether universally beloved or feared, admired or mocked, I've come to believe that every bird has a story to tell.

So, the next time you see a cardinal at your bird feeder or a hawk soaring overhead, consider what message it may have for you. What wisdom does it carry? What secrets might it confide?

# BIRDS

# THE ALBATROSS

*Diomedeidae*

**Meaning:** Guilt, A burden

**Lore:** In *The Rime of the Ancient Mariner,* Samuel Taylor Coleridge's narrative poem, a sailor kills an albatross with his crossbow. This sets off a series of distressing events, leading the crew of the ship to believe the killing of the bird cursed their voyage. They tie the albatross around the sailor's neck as punishment and to remind him of his mistake. A large bird, the albatross's weight would have been difficult to bear. For this reason, the bird is associated with heavy, inescapable burdens—especially those of a psychological nature.

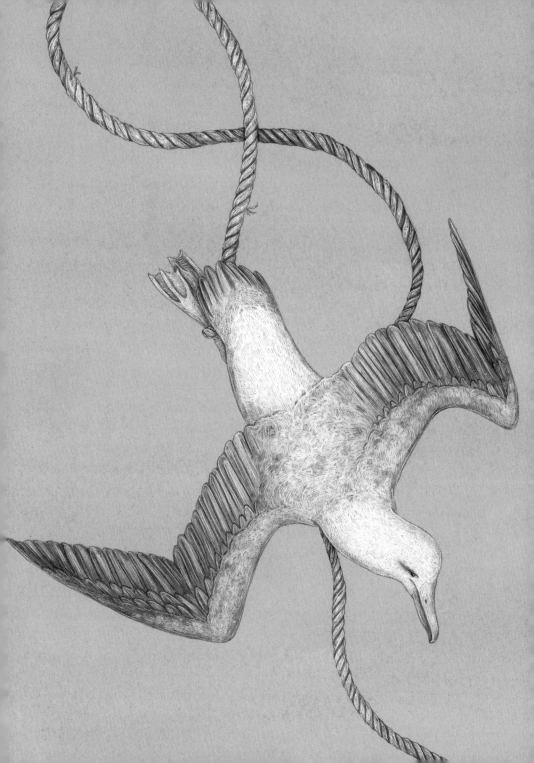

# THE AMERICAN ROBIN

*Turdus migratorius*

**Meaning:** Hope

**Lore:** In colder parts of North America, the first sight of a robin after a long winter is a symbol of hope for the coming warmth of spring.

The shíshálh people tell a story of how the robin got his red breast. During a cold winter when the world was new, the young men left their tribe's cave to find food and wood for the fire. An elder man watched the fire and carefully kept it going for the tribe, but after many days awake, he fell asleep, and the fire began to go out. A gray robin saw that the fire was fading and beat his wings to keep it alive, burning his chest feathers bright orange in the process. The bird saved the people from freezing in the night, and the hunters returned the following day with food and firewood.

# THE ARCTIC TERN

*Sterna paradisaea*

**Meaning:** Travels

**Lore:** These striking black, white, and gray seabirds with red bills hold the record for the longest migration in the animal kingdom. They fly from the Arctic, where they breed, to Antarctica, where they summer every year, a span of around forty-four thousand miles for the birds that nest in Iceland and Greenland. Arctic terns that nest in the Netherlands have a slightly shorter journey of around thirty thousand miles—still a shocking feat. It's no wonder these tenacious birds are well-known travelers.

# THE BITTERN

*Botaurinae*

**Meaning:** Fear of the unknown

**Lore:** Difficult to spot due to their striped, camouflaging feathers, these marshland birds are known for their booming call.

In Slavic folklore, the call of the bittern is associated with the *drekavac,* a mythical graveyard creature known for its distinctive screech. Branko Ćopić's "Brave Mita and Drekavac from the Pond" tells of fishermen who, after hearing what they believe to be the *drekavac* in their fishing territory, cease fishing and leave the villagers to starve. A local boy named Mita investigates the haunting sounds, discovering that their true source is the bittern.

Similarly, in Sir Arthur Conan Doyle's *The Hound of the Baskervilles,* one character suggests that the low, howling sound on the moors may be "the cry of the last of the bitterns."

**See also:** *The Egret (page 52), The Heron (page 74)*

# THE BLACKBIRD

*Turdus merula*

**Meaning:** Transformation

**Lore:** In Italy, the *giorni della merla* ("blackbird days") are the coldest days of the year, at the end of January. A popular Italian legend claims that blackbirds were once all white. During the coldest days of winter, the birds sought refuge in chimneys, where their feathers were blackened by soot. Though they are rare, albino (all white) and leucistic (black and white) blackbirds do appear from time to time, perhaps contributing to this lore.

# THE BLUE JAY

*Cyanocitta cristata*

**Meaning:** Treachery

**Lore:** In the antebellum American South, the noisy and aggressive blue jay was said to be a traveler between our world and hell, bringing sticks to fuel hellfire each Friday. The bird itself was not considered evil; rather, it had been cursed by the devil as the result of an ill-fated deal and attempted betrayal. Other stories tell of the blue jay bringing grains of sand to the underworld as ransom for the souls residing there. Always an intermediary creature, the blue jay flies the line between cunning and deceit.

# THE BLUEBIRD

*Sialia*

**Meaning:** Patience, Hope

**Lore:** The French fairy tale "The Blue Bird" by Madame d'Aulnoy tells the love story of Florine and King Charming. Florine's stepmother locks her in a tower while she attempts to persuade the visiting king to marry her own daughter—Florine's stepsister. When he refuses, having fallen in love with Florine at first sight, the queen curses him, transforming him into a bluebird. In his bird form, he visits Florine in her tower, bringing her jewels and singing his song of love. Many years later, after the death of her father and stepmother, Florine is freed and becomes queen. She searches for and finds King Charming, who has regained his human form thanks to a kind enchanter, and the two wed, fulfilling their long-deferred love.

# THE BOOBY

*Sula*

**Meaning:** Curiosity

**Lore:** In the sixteenth century, these striking birds often landed on the ships of Spanish sailors exploring the Pacific coast and islands of Central and South America. Because the naive birds were easily captured and eaten, the sailors nicknamed them *bobo*—slang at the time for "foolish." The moniker stuck, perhaps helped by the birds' awkward gait on land. Despite the name, boobies are in fact intelligent birds and are even graceful in air and on water. Likely never having seen such vessels, they approached the Spanish ships with an understandable (but ill-fated) curiosity.

# THE BOWERBIRD

*Ptilonorhynchidae*

**Meaning:** Artistry

**Lore:** The male bowerbird is known for his elaborately crafted archway, or "bower," used to entice females to mate with him. Found in Australia and New Guinea, the bowerbird is the architect of the avian kingdom, creating an artful tunnel that leads to a decorated court full of carefully selected items arranged by color and shape. The male performs within the court, strutting and vocalizing, and the female bowerbird may accept his advances only if she is impressed.

# THE CALIFORNIA CONDOR

*Gymnogyps californianus*

**Meaning:** A new beginning

**Lore:** The critically endangered California condor is the largest North American land bird. Venerated by many Native American peoples, the bird is included in numerous creation stories.

The Wiyot people believe that the condor is the life giver from which all peoples descend. In the Wiyot creation myth, the condor and his sister are the only survivors of a great flood that covered the earth, marking a new beginning for humanity.

Today, many Native American tribes, notably the Yurok, are involved in giving the condor its own new beginning. Threatened by habitat destruction, poaching, and poisoning, the legendary bird is now among the rarest on Earth.

# THE CANARY

*Serinus*

**Meaning:** A warning

**Lore:** The phrase "canary in a coal mine" refers to the use of caged canaries in mines during the early twentieth century. Because the birds are much more sensitive than humans to carbon monoxide and other toxic gases, their behavior could warn miners of dangerous conditions. If the bird perished or became agitated, it gave workers enough time to get aboveground before being harmed themselves.

# THE CARDINAL

*Cardinalis*

**Meaning:** Confidence

**Lore:** Bright-red male cardinals are named after Catholic cardinals, high-ranking church dignitaries who wear red robes to signify their importance. The name "cardinal" comes from the Latin *cardo,* meaning "hinge": something or someone upon which another depends. Like a red-robed clergyman acting decisively and with authority, these regal birds exude a powerful confidence.

# THE CASSOWARY

*Casuarius*

**Meaning:** Defying expectations

**Lore:** A large, flightless bird, the cassowary plays an important role in Australian Aboriginal traditional stories. One tale of Dreamtime—the summary term for world-creation beliefs in Aboriginal religion and culture—tells of how the bird got his unusual hornlike head crest, called a casque: The poor bird was mocked by the other animals for having small wings and being unable to fly. One day, while fleeing his bullies, the cassowary ran into a rock, breaking it into pieces, one of which stuck to the top of his head. Everyone laughed at the bird, and he withdrew even further from the community. But when a group of snakes attacked, the cassowary heard the cries of the other animals and came to their rescue, using his casque to push away the predators. From then on, he was celebrated as a hero.

# THE CATBIRD

*Dumetella carolinensis*

**Meaning:** Advantage

**Lore:** A member of the Mimidae family along with mockingbirds and thrashers, the gray catbird is aptly named: its call sounds just like a meowing cat. Because catbirds tend to sing from high and exposed perches, they have come to be associated with advantage. The idiom "in the catbird seat," coined in the American South to describe someone in a position of power or control, was popularized by early twentieth-century baseball announcer Red Barber, who claimed to have heard it while playing poker.

**See also:** *The Mockingbird (page 106), The Thrasher (page 180)*

# THE CHICKADEE

*Poecile*

**Meaning:** Honesty

**Lore:** The humble chickadee is revered in Cherokee legend as an honest messenger. One folktale tells of an evil, shapeshifting witch called Spearfinger, named for the long, stony finger she used to attack anyone who got too close. Try as they might, the villagers were unable to destroy her—that is, until a chickadee revealed that the witch's heart was located in her sharp finger. A hunter aimed his arrow at the witch's finger, killing her and confirming the helpful chickadee's trustworthiness.

**See also:** *The Titmouse (page 184)*

# THE COOT

*Fulica*

**Meaning:** Tenacity

**Lore:** The coot looks a bit like a cross between a chicken and a duck, with dark plumage, a rounded body, and large feet.

The Nüwa people of modern-day California say that the coot, or the Earth Diver, existed in a time when only water covered the globe. All the animals and birds tried to dive down to the bottom of the sea to bring up dirt to create the land, but only the coot was successful. The bird's tenacious efforts produced the terrain we walk on today.

# THE CORMORANT

*Phalacrocorax*

**Meaning:** Good luck, Victory

**Lore:** A large black seabird, the cormorant features in folklore from around the world, typically symbolizing victory over death. In Homer's *Odyssey*, a sea nymph disguises herself as a cormorant and helps a shipwrecked Odysseus make it to shore. Similarly, in Norwegian folklore, it is said that the spirits of those lost at sea return to their loved ones in the form of cormorants. Associated with strength and good fortune, the bird is also a common heraldic symbol, appearing in many European coats of arms.

# THE COWBIRD

*Molothrus*

**Meaning:** Stealth

**Lore:** The cowbird's scientific name, *Molothrus,* is a combination of the Greek words meaning "struggle" or "battle" and "to impregnate," alluding to its habit of laying eggs in other birds' nests. Like some cuckoos, the female cowbird does not build her own nest; instead, she observes potential surrogate mothers and lays her egg in the nest of one she's confident will care for her hatchling. When she does this, the cowbird may secretly remove or destroy one of the surrogate mother's eggs, making room for her own.

**See also:** *The Cuckoo (page 42)*

# THE CRANE

*Grus*

**Meaning:** Fortune

**Lore:** The crane's graceful beauty has given rise to dozens of myths. In Japan, where it is rumored that cranes live for a thousand years, the birds are revered as symbols of fortune and longevity.

In the story of "Tsuru no ongaeshi," meaning "the crane's return of a favor," a poor man nurses an injured crane back to life. After the bird is healed and flies away, the man finds a beautiful woman, who becomes his wife. She tells her husband not to come into her room until she is finished creating something that will make them wealthy. After a week, she presents him with a beautiful weaving—but she appears to be ill. He sells the weaving, and she begins to make another. This time, he looks in on her, breaking his promise not to enter her room, and sees that she is the same crane he rescued. She has been disguising herself as a woman and using her own feathers to weave beautiful silks for him to sell. She tells him she can no longer stay with him now that he has discovered her secret.

**See also:** *The Emu (page 54)*

# THE CROW

*Corvus*

**Meaning:** Cleverness

**Lore:** Crows are known around the world for their intelligence and cunning. In Aesop's Fables, an ancient Greek collection of moralistic tales, a thirsty crow comes upon a jar containing water, but the jar has a long neck, and the bird can't reach the liquid inside. Knowing if the jar tips over that the water will be spilled and wasted, the crow comes up with a brilliant plan: he drops pebbles into the jar one by one, displacing the water so that it rises nearer the opening. Finally able to take a sip, the clever bird quenches his thirst.

**See also:** *The Magpie (page 104), The Raven (page 154)*

# THE CUCKOO

*Cuculus*

**Meaning:** Duplicity

**Lore:** Like the cowbird, the parasitic cuckoo is known for hiding her eggs in the nests of other bird species. Hatchling cuckoos will then push the competing chicks out of the nest and enjoy nourishment from the unsuspecting parents.

The term "cuckold" derives from the cuckoo. Most often, it refers to a man whose wife has been unfaithful to him, but originally, the term could be applied to an adulterer of either sex. For example, in Greek mythology, Zeus, king of the ancient Greek gods, turns himself into a cuckoo to woo the goddess Hera. The two wed, but Zeus is a notorious philanderer who fathers several children with other goddesses, nymphs, and mortal women.

**See also:** *The Cowbird (page 36)*

# THE DODO

*Raphus cucullatus*

**Meaning:** Obsolescence

**Lore:** The dodo was a flightless bird from Mauritius that became extinct in the seventeenth century due to overhunting and habitat loss. The bird was once well-adapted to its environment, with few natural predators and a wealth of food sources. However, following the arrival of the Dutch on the island in 1598, the number of dodos began to dwindle, and by the 1660s, they had died out completely.

Today, we say that something has "gone the way of the dodo" to mean that it has become obsolete. The fate of these birds is a tragic reminder of how quickly human activity can destroy a species.

# THE DOVE

*Streptopelia risoria*

**Meaning:** Love, Hope

**Lore:** The biblical story of Noah's Ark conjures the image of a white dove carrying an olive branch in its beak, an iconic symbol of hope. After many weeks at sea, Noah sends a dove out to look for land. When the bird returns with an olive branch, Noah knows the floodwaters are receding and he will soon find safe harbor. In Christian art, the Holy Spirit often takes the form of a dove.

Earlier cultures associated the dove with love. It was a symbol of Astarte, the goddess of love and war in ancient Mesopotamia, as well as Aphrodite, the Greek goddess of love.

# THE DUCK

*Anatidae*

**Meaning:** Transfiguration

**Lore:** Ducks appear in many children's stories, but perhaps most iconically in Hans Christian Andersen's "The Ugly Duckling"— a tale in which an unusual-looking duckling is relentlessly teased by his siblings. After much hardship, the duckling finds himself welcomed into a flock of wild swans. Seeing his reflection in the water, he realizes that he is not a duck at all but a swan.

Folklore featuring ducks confused for swans (and vice versa) abounds, perhaps because the two species belong to the Anatidae family of waterbirds. Interestingly, in another of Andersen's stories, "The Wild Swans," he modifies a traditional Norwegian tale. In the original, twelve boys are transformed into ducks, but in Andersen's version, there are eleven boys, and they become swans. In both stories, the boys' sister works to restore their human form.

**See also:** *The Swan (page 176)*

# THE EAGLE

*Accipitridae*

**Meaning:** Strength, Focus

**Lore:** Reverence for these large birds of prey appears in folklore and history from around the world. A well-known symbol in American and European heraldry, the eagle's association with strength may derive from its connection to the Greek god Zeus. He was said to favor the bird for its perceived strength and power.

The Roman naturalist Pliny the Elder took this a step further, writing that eagles were able to look directly at the sun without blinking and trained their offspring to do the same—hence the term "eagle-eyed," meaning highly observant and attuned to small details.

Early Christian writers also associated the eagle with strength, emphasizing its ability to ascend heavenward. The eagle became a symbol of Saint John the Evangelist, whose gospel was thought to have a soaring, inspirational quality.

# THE EGRET

*Ardeinae*

**Meaning:** Rare beauty

**Lore:** Egrets, a type of heron, have elegant long legs and glistening white feathers. In Maori culture, the great egret—called the kotuku—is a symbol of rare beauty. Because only 150 to 200 egrets nest in New Zealand, the Maori coined the phrase "rare as the kotuku" to describe a remarkably beautiful person. Another phrase, *te kotuku rerenga tahi,* translates to "the egret of a single flight" and refers to esteemed guests who seldom visit. To spot a kotuku, or to be called one, is considered a blessing in Maori tradition.

**See also:** *The Bittern (page 8), The Heron (page 74)*

# THE EMU

*Dromaius novaehollandiae*

**Meaning:** Celestial guidance

**Lore:** The national bird of Australia, the towering emu holds a prominent place in Aboriginal culture and Dreamtime folklore. The dark bands of the Milky Way are said to depict an "emu in the sky," and diverse tales from various peoples tell of how the emu came to appear there.

Another story relates how the emu egg became the sun: An argument broke out between Dinewan, an emu, and Brolga, a crane. Brolga threw an egg from Dinewan's nest into the sky, and the yolk of the egg transformed into the sun.

**See also:** *The Crane (page 38), The Ostrich (page 118), The Rhea (page 156)*

# THE EUROPEAN ROBIN

*Erithacus rubecula*

**Meaning:** Compassion

**Lore:** So beloved are these birds that to harm or kill a European robin is to invite a curse. In Norse mythology, the robin was sacred to Thor—the god of thunder—and he was said to strike with lightning anyone who hurt the bird or its nest. An old British rhyme references this idea:

> *The robin and the wren*
>
> *Are God Almighty's cock and hen*
>
> *Him that harries their nest*
>
> *Never shall his soul have rest.*

Later British folktales suggest that the robin's breast was stained red by the blood of Jesus as he was crucified. The robin sang to comfort him and, in some stories, attempted to remove his crown of thorns.

**See also:** *The Wren (page 200)*

# THE FINCH

*Fringillidae*

**Meaning:** Domesticity

**Lore:** Appreciated for their charming feathers and joyous chirps, finches have long been kept as pets. Dexterous creatures, they can be taught to perform tricks, such as ringing a bell or lifting a small bucket of food or water on a string.

Goldfinches in particular appear frequently in Renaissance depictions of the Madonna and child. They were a favorite household pet at the time, often given to children.

# THE FLAMINGO

*Phoenicopteridae*

**Meaning:** Survival

**Lore:** These iconic pink birds may explain the origin of the mythological phoenix. "Flamingo" comes from the Latin *flamma*, meaning "flame." In ancient times, travelers to the Great Rift Valley in eastern Africa would occasionally see these large reddish birds through the thick, steamy mists of near-boiling volcanic lakes. The creatures were even known to drink the caustic lake water. Reports of these "fire birds" were passed on to the Greeks and eventually made their way throughout Europe, perhaps inspiring the tale of the phoenix, a bird said to burst into flames and then reemerge from its own ashes.

# THE GANNET

*Morus*

**Meaning:** A gift

**Lore:** The gannet, a seabird with a voracious appetite, is often found on islands and coasts. In the Faeroe Islands, the myth of the three gifts for Mykines tells of the importance of gannets as a food source. After islander Óli defeats the giant Tórur Rami, Tórur gives him and the island three gifts, which they can keep as long as they do not laugh at them. The first is the bottlenose whale, the second is driftwood, and the third is the gannet. Óli and the islanders mock the whale and driftwood, but they accept the gift of the gannet, considered a delicacy.

# THE GOOSE

*Anser*

**Meaning:** Wealth

**Lore:** To "kill the goose that lays the golden egg" is to shortsightedly destroy one's source of prosperity. The phrase derives from Aesop's Fables, but legends of waterfowl laying golden eggs can be found in many cultures. In Aesop's tale, a couple kills their goose that lays golden eggs, thinking the bird itself must be made of gold. Instead, they are left with an ordinary dead goose and no more golden eggs.

In an earlier Hindu myth, the creator god Brahma is said to have been born from a golden egg, and he is often depicted riding a goose. Ancient Egyptians, too, told of a creator god who took the form of a goose that laid a golden egg. When the egg hatched, it became the sun. These legends likely influenced Aesop's allegory.

# THE GRACKLE

*Quiscalus*

**Meaning:** Intrusion

**Lore:** Loud black birds with dazzling iridescent plumage, grackles are known to devastate crops with their fondness for grain. For this reason, they are most often seen as pests. Indeed, a flock of grackles is called a plague, referencing the damage a group of these birds can quickly inflict.

Grackles weren't always seen as a nuisance, however. In the late 1400s, the Aztec emperor Ahuitzotl was so enamored of great-tailed grackles that he demanded they be brought from the area of modern-day Veracruz to the Valley of Mexico, the center of the empire. They were considered sacred and called *teotzanatl,* meaning "divine grackle."

# THE GULL

*Laridae*

**Meaning:** Duality

**Lore:** These coastal birds with webbed feet can be found on every continent. Creatures of the shoreline, gulls feed both on land and at sea.

A Welsh myth illustrates the gull's duality: The sea god Dylan envies an old man with three beautiful daughters. To claim them for himself, Dylan calls up a great storm, sweeping the women away. However, seeing their father's heartbreak, Dylan transforms the sisters into seagulls, allowing them to travel between land and sea.

# THE HARPY EAGLE

*Harpia harpyja*

**Meaning:** Cruelty

**Lore:** Found in Central and South America, the harpy eagle, named for the mythic harpies of ancient Greece, is a massive, powerful raptor with eerily humanlike facial features. Half-bird, half-woman, the harpies were a type of destructive wind spirit later tasked with bringing souls to the underworld. According to legend, they were foul-smelling creatures, seen as cruel and violent.

Despite their namesake, harpy eagles are not cruel birds. Ironically, they are the target of human cruelty. Today, conservationists seek to end violence against these raptors, which are frequently hunted for their meat and captured for illegal trade.

# THE HAWK

*Accipitridae*

**Meaning:** Intensity

**Lore:** Hawks are large birds of prey often associated with—or confused for—falcons. Falconry was once called hawking, and the two birds are seen as interchangeable in many cultures. Likewise, their folklore frequently overlaps. For example, the ancient Egyptian god Horus is described as hawk- or falcon-headed, depending on the source.

Fierce predators, red-tailed hawks can reach speeds of over 120 miles per hour while diving to catch their prey. It is no surprise, then, that Circe, a tempestuous Greek goddess best known for exacting swift and devastating revenge, has a name meaning "circling hawk."

**See also:** *The Peregrine Falcon (page 132)*

# THE HERON

*Ardeidae*

**Meaning:** A positive message

**Lore:** With its long, elegant legs and neck, the heron is closely related to the bittern, and the two species often overlap in mythology.

The ancient Egyptian deity Bennu is depicted as a large heron. In one creation myth, he is said to fly over the waters of Nu, land on a rock, and cry out, calling forth life itself. Bennu was likely inspired by a now-extinct species of giant herons that were roughly the size of adult humans.

Herons were also associated with the Greek goddess Athena. In Homer's *Iliad,* Athena sends a heron to Diomedes and Odysseus as a symbol of good luck. When they hear the cry of the bird, they pray to Athena.

**See also:** *The Bittern (page 8), The Egret (page 52)*

# THE HORNBILL

*Bucerotidae*

**Meaning:** Consolation

**Lore:** Hornbills are named for their distinctive large bills, and some species have a casque, or head crest, making them valuable targets for poachers. The most iconic hornbill in popular culture might be Zazu from Disney's *The Lion King*, but these birds have been mythologized for thousands of years.

In the northeastern Indian state of Nagaland, the yearly Hornbill Festival celebrates these birds as sacred spiritual beings. One Sumi Naga folktale tells of two lovers, Kivigho and Kahuli. While walking to their village, Kahuli became hungry, so Kivigho climbed a fruit tree for her—but the branches he used to ascend the tree broke off as he climbed, making it impossible for him to get back down. Resigned to his fate, Kivigho transformed himself into a great hornbill and dropped one of his feathers into Kahuli's lap. She treasured the reminder of her lover for the rest of her life. To commemorate this myth, members of various Naga peoples still use hornbill feathers in their traditional headdresses.

# THE HUMMINGBIRD

*Trochilidae*

**Meaning:** Might

**Lore:** Glittering hummingbirds are named for the sound their wings make as they flutter rapidly. Small but mighty, these birds were revered by the Aztecs. Huitzilopochtli, the god of sun and war, was often depicted as a hummingbird or with a hummingbird-shaped helmet. Warriors who died in battle and women who died during childbirth were said to transform into hummingbirds and join Huitzilopochtli in the afterlife. Dead hummingbirds were even carried by warriors into battle as good-luck charms.

# THE IBIS

*Threskiornithinae*

**Meaning:** Knowledge

**Lore:** Often found near bodies of water, the ibis is a large, graceful bird with a distinctive, downwardly curved beak. Its scientific subfamily name, Threskiornithinae, comes from the ancient Greek words for "sacred bird."

The ancient Egyptian deity Thoth was depicted as a man with the head of an ibis. Also known as Djehuty, meaning "he who is like the ibis," he was the god of knowledge, specifically in writing and mathematics. In Hermopolis, the city dedicated to worshipping Thoth, ibises were so revered, they were mummified alongside pharaohs.

# THE JACANA

*Jacanidae*

**Meaning:** A miracle

**Lore:** Jacana's long, slim toes allow them to balance on lily pads and other floating vegetation, giving the appearance of walking on water. Because of this, they are sometimes called "Jesus birds," in reference to the biblical story in which Jesus walks on the Sea of Galilee.

Jacana young are cared for by their fathers, who scoop them up in their wings and carry them away whenever danger approaches. This causes the adult males to appear to have many spindly legs, a bit like a supernatural half spider, half bird.

# THE JUNCO

*Junco*

**Meaning:** Winter

**Lore:** The dark-eyed junco, a close relative of the sparrow, is a small bird with a very small genus. Commonly called "snowbirds," juncos arrive at the backyard bird feeder to signal the start of winter. These diminutive birds are not bothered by winds or snow; they thrive in cold weather.

When spring comes, they escape the thaw by flying to higher elevations.

**See also:** *The Sparrow (page 166)*

# THE KINGFISHER

*Alcedinidae*

**Meaning:** Devotion

**Lore:** Beautiful, brightly colored birds with long, pointed beaks, kingfishers are noted for their fishing ability. The Greek *alkyōn* or "halcyon," meaning "kingfisher," refers to the myth of Ceyx and Alcyone.

Alcyone was the wife of Ceyx, King of Trachis, and the two were deeply in love. They were known to call each other "Zeus" and "Hera" in jest, but this sacrilege angered Zeus. While Ceyx was at sea, Zeus sent a thunderbolt to destroy his ship, killing him. When Ceyx did not return, Alcyone was distraught. Hera, seeing Alcyone's suffering, took pity on her and sent Morpheus, the god of dreams, to tell her what had happened to Ceyx. In her grief, Alcyone threw herself into the sea to be reunited with her husband. Out of compassion for the couple, the gods turned them both into kingfishers.

**See also:** *The Kookaburra (page 92)*

# THE KITE

*Milvus migrans*

**Meaning:** Mourning

**Lore:** These scavenging birds of prey are associated with the ancient Egyptian goddess Isis, who is often depicted with the wings of a kite.

According to legend, when Isis's husband, Osiris, was killed by his jealous brother, she turned herself and her sister, Nephthys, into black kites. Just as a kite would search for carrion, the two women scavenged for Osiris's remains. Eventually, Isis was able to collect Osiris's parts and make him whole again, fanning her wings to bring him back to life.

The call of a black kite is noted for its shrillness, and ancient Egyptians believed its wailing cries were those of the bereft Isis, searching for her husband.

# THE KIWI

*Apteryx*

**Meaning:** Sacrifice

**Lore:** The national bird of New Zealand, the kiwi is a small flightless bird resembling the fruit of the same name, as its hairlike feathers take after the fur on a kiwifruit's skin.

A Maori legend explains how the kiwi lost its ability to fly. Tāne Mahuta, the father of the forest, discovered that insects were eating his trees and making them ill. He called upon his brother, Tāne Hokahoka, the god of the birds, for help. Together, they asked if a bird would come down from the sky and live on the forest floor to eat the destructive insects. Only the brave kiwi agreed. Although he knew this meant he would never fly again, he chose to protect the forest.

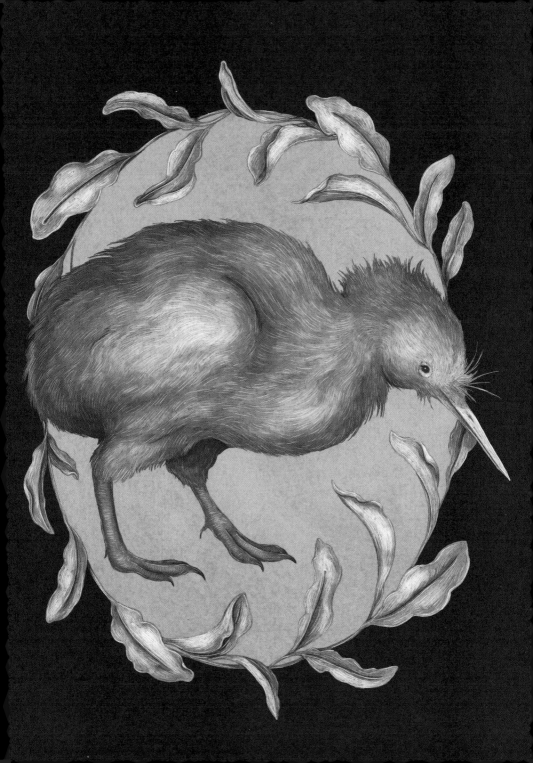

# THE KOOKABURRA

*Dacelo*

**Meaning:** Joy

**Lore:** The kookaburra is a type of Australian kingfisher known for its loud, laughter-like call. According to Aboriginal mythology, the creator deity Baiame commanded these birds to call out during the first sunrise so that mankind and the creatures of the world would not miss the sight. To this day, the kookaburra "laughs" mirthfully at the rising sun.

**See also:** *The Kingfisher (page 86)*

# THE LAPWING

*Vanellinae*

**Meaning:** Deceit

**Lore:** Lapwings, occasionally mistaken for plovers, are ground-nesting birds with an unfortunate reputation. A group of lapwings is called a deceit, and the folklore surrounding these waders suggests why.

Swedish legend tells of a servant to the Virgin Mary who fled after stealing a pair of scissors. When caught, the servant was turned into a lapwing: a bird whose tail feathers appear to be severed. What's more, the call of the lapwing sounds like "*Tyvit! Tyvit!*" which translates from Swedish as "I stole! I stole!"

**See also:** *The Plover (page 142)*

# THE LARK

*Alaudidae*

**Meaning:** Levity

**Lore:** Larks are known for their cheerful, melodious song. Singing even while in flight, these birds have come to be associated with carefree joy, as reflected in the phrases "happy as a lark," meaning joyful, and "on a lark," meaning on a whim or in a spirit of fun and playfulness. The lark also lends its name to the larkspur, a flower whose unique seedhead resembles the bird's foot. Taking after its namesake, the larkspur symbolizes levity in the Victorian language of flowers.

Shakespeare often references larks as carefree and happy creatures, perhaps most notably in *The Winter's Tale*, in the breezy song of Autolycus:

> *The lark, that tirralirra chants,*
>
> *With heigh, with heigh, the thrush and the jay,*
>
> *Are summer songs for me and my aunts,*
>
> *While we lie tumbling in the hay.*

# THE LITTLE OWL

*Athene noctua*

**Meaning:** Wisdom

**Lore:** Sacred to Athena, Greek goddess of wisdom, the little owl is noted for its innate intelligence and uncanny ability to see in the dark. In ancient Athens, the sight of an owl was believed to be a favorable sign from Athena, who was often depicted with this bird by her side.

A Victorian-era British nursery rhyme, "A Wise Old Owl," describes one who displays both keen listening and discretion:

> *There was an owl liv'd in an oak*
>
> *The more he heard, the less he spoke*
>
> *The less he spoke, the more he heard.*
>
> *O, if men were all like that wise bird.*

# THE LOON

*Gavia*

**Meaning:** A helping hand

**Lore:** Excellent swimmers with unique black-and-white markings and haunting red eyes, loons trace their meaning to a Tsimshian legend from the Pacific Northwest coast of North America. An old man who had recently gone blind went to the lake to sing about his misery; without his sight, he could no longer gather food for his family. When the loon heard his song, it told the man to mount its back and bury his face in its feathers. The loon dove beneath the water's surface twice, and when the pair emerged, the man had regained his sight. In thanks, he gave the loon his precious shell necklace, which the bird has worn ever since: a band of white against the dark plumage of its neck.

# THE LYREBIRD

*Menura*

**Meaning:** Mentorship

**Lore:** The lyrebird is named for the male bird's tail feathers, which resemble a lyre—a small stringed instrument similar to a harp. The lyrebird is also noted for its ability to mimic the calls of other birds.

An Aboriginal Dreamtime story tells of a lyrebird who sings at a bubbling stream. The bird notices one bubble that dances along to his song. Recognizing a spirit who wants to come to life, the lyrebird watches as the bubble hatches into a little green frog. The bird takes the frog under his wing, teaching the creature to sing.

# THE MAGPIE

*Pica*

**Meaning:** Prophecy

**Lore:** Loud, chattering birds with lustrous black-and-white plumage, magpies belong to the corvid family; like the crow and raven, they are known for their intelligence, strident call, and association with superstition. The eighteenth-century British nursery rhyme "One for Sorrow" explained what it meant to see a magpie— or two or three. Most modern versions go something like this:

> *One for sorrow,*
>
> *Two for joy,*
>
> *Three for a girl,*
>
> *Four for a boy,*
>
> *Five for silver,*
>
> *Six for gold,*
>
> *Seven for a secret never to be told.*

**See also:** *The Crow (page 40), The Raven (page 154)*

# THE MOCKINGBIRD

*Mimus polyglottos*

**Meaning:** Innocence

**Lore:** The northern mockingbird's species name means "many tongues" and references its mimicry skills, which result in a diverse array of calls. Beloved by gardeners, these musical birds are known to eat pests but leave fruits and vegetables untouched.

In Harper Lee's famous 1960 novel, *To Kill A Mockingbird*, the titular bird becomes a symbol of innocence. In the story, Miss Maudie Atkinson explains why it's a sin to kill mockingbirds: "They don't do one thing but sing their hearts out for us." The passage is considered a metaphor for the plight of the wrongly accused, especially victims of prejudice.

**See also:** *The Catbird (page 28), The Thrasher (page 180)*

# THE NIGHTINGALE

*Luscinia megarhynchos*

**Meaning:** Unrequited love

**Lore:** Persian lore describes the rose and nightingale as symbols of perfection and beauty. Lovers who can never meet, the pair is ultimately doomed, for the rigid thorns of the perfect rose will pierce the passionate bird as they embrace.

In Oscar Wilde's story "The Nightingale and the Rose," a student laments that the woman he loves won't dance with him unless he brings her a red rose. Overhearing this, a nearby nightingale asks a rose tree for a blossom. The tree has no blooms, but it tells the bird to sing through the night with a rose thorn piercing her heart. The nightingale does so, giving her life so that a single red rose will appear. In the morning, the student plucks the flower and offers it to his beloved, but she rejects it. Distraught, the student tosses the rose in the gutter, vowing never to pursue love again.

# THE NIGHTJAR

*Caprimulgidae*

**Meaning:** A false accusation

**Lore:** Sometimes called nighthawks or goatsuckers, these nocturnal birds have short bills, large black eyes, and an unflattering reputation. According to Aristotle, the nightjar was thought to suckle milk from goats at night, causing the animals to stop lactating and go blind. While nightjars do tend to congregate around goats after sundown, they do so to eat the insects the livestock stir up—not to drink their milk.

# THE NUTHATCH

*Sitta*

**Meaning:** Ingenuity

**Lore:** The nuthatch is named for its ingenious ability to crack nuts by wedging them into crevices and hammering them with its bill. In his *History of Animals,* Aristotle describes this shrewd skill and notes that the nuthatch and eagle are enemies. The nuthatch, he claims, with its strong beak, "hatches" the eagle's eggs, destroying his adversary's offspring. While we can thank Aristotle for noting the bird's ingenuity, this particular behavior has not been otherwise observed.

# THE ORIOLE

*Icteridae, Oriolidae*

**Meaning:** Musicality

**Lore:** Sightly songbirds with yellow and black plumage, the common name "oriole" applies to two unrelated groups of birds: *Icteridae*, found in the Americas, and *Oriolidae*, found in Europe, Africa, Asia, and Australia. Esteemed for its music, the black-naped oriole appeared on decorative badges, called mandarin squares, of high-ranking court officials in China during the Ming dynasty (1368–1644). In the 1760s, during the Qing dynasty, they were adopted as the symbol for court musicians.

# THE OSPREY

*Pandion haliaetus*

**Meaning:** Ferocity

**Lore:** A large raptor whose name derives from the Latin *ossifraga*, meaning "bone breaker," the osprey appears in various myths and legends, often as a ferocious predator.

The bird's impressive fishing skills were recorded by a thirteenth-century Dominican friar and "Doctor of the Church," Albertus Magnus, who believed the osprey had one webbed foot for swimming and one sharply clawed talon for catching prey. Although this is not factual, the bird does have large hooked talons and barbs on the pads of its feet, perfect for capturing slippery fish.

# THE OSTRICH

*Struthio*

**Meaning:** Strength

**Lore:** The largest, heaviest, and fastest-running land bird on Earth, the ostrich cannot fly but is noted for its legendary strength. So impressed was Pliny the Elder by these mammoth birds that he claimed they could eat "every substance without distinction." Many more legends developed, including a medieval myth describing the bird's ability to hatch its eggs by staring at them intently.

Even more storied than the ostrich, however, are its massive eggs, the yolks of which are equivalent in terms of size and nutrition to that of about twenty-four chicken eggs. As early as 4000 BCE, ostrich eggs were hollowed out, occasionally carved with intricate designs, and used as perfume containers and drinking cups. In ancient Egypt, the eggs fed pharaohs and were included in funeral rites, and in ancient Greece and Rome, they were offered to deities.

**See also:** *The Emu (page 54), The Rhea (page 156)*

118

# THE OWL

*Strigiformes*

**Meaning:** An ill omen

**Lore:** Nocturnal birds with haunting cries, owls are regarded as harbingers of evil and even death in many cultures. Chaucer noted this in *The Parliament of Fowls,* stating, "The owl too, that portent of death does bring." Shakespeare echoed the sentiment in *Henry VI, Part 3*: "The owl shrieked at thy birth, an evil sign." But the association of owls with ill omens isn't exclusively Western; the Kikuyu people of Kenya believe the bird's call warns of impending death.

Owls have often been associated with witchcraft. For example, the ancient Romans believed that the Strix or Striges were witches who could transform into owl-like creatures to feed on human blood. The order Strigiformes takes its name from these malevolent beasts.

# THE PARAKEET

*Psittacula longicauda*

**Meaning:** Reunion

**Lore:** The long-tailed parakeet is an attractive bird with green, red, and blue plumage. In a folktale from northern Sumatra, Indonesia, a group of parakeets is captured by a hunter. The king of the parakeets convinces his flock to play dead so that the hunter will release them. The ruse works, and all of the parakeets manage to escape—except for the king, who is taken to a palace and enclosed in a golden cage. The parakeet king is devastated, but he hatches another plan: he stops eating, stops singing, and pretends to be seriously ill to convince his captors he is dying. When his cage is opened, he flies out and is reunited with his flock.

# THE PARROT

*Psittaciformes*

**Meaning:** Bravery

**Lore:** Large and exceptionally colorful birds, parrots have long captured the human imagination. According to a South Asian legend, the Buddha was once born as a small gray parrot. When a storm sparked a wildfire in his forest, the parrot began dipping himself in the river and desperately shaking his wings over the flames. Seeing this, a god of the heavens was moved by the little parrot's efforts to save the forest. The god wept, and his tears extinguished the blaze. Charred by flames and doused in tears, the once homely parrot became an exquisite, brightly colored bird: red for the fire, blue for the water, green for the forest, and yellow for the sun.

# THE PEACOCK

*Pavo cristatus*

**Meaning:** Reverence

**Lore:** The peacock, unlike the modest female peahen, is a showy and stately bird revered as sacred in a number of cultures.

In the Middle Eastern Yazidi religion, Tawûsî Melek (Kurdish for "Peacock Angel") is the leader of God's seven angels. He is responsible for all that occurs in nature—the earth, sky, mountains, and sea.

In ancient Greece, the peacock was sacred to Hera and pulled the goddess's chariot. The ancient Greeks, who believed peacocks did not decay after death, associated these birds with immortality.

The Sanskrit word for peacock—*mayura*—is associated with many Hindu gods; the peacock is also the national bird of India, which is its home country. In one legend, Indra, the Hindu god of rain, was fighting the demon Ravana when a peacock shielded him by hiding him from view. To thank the bird, Indra gave him beautiful blue-green feathers.

# THE PELICAN

*Pelecanus*

**Meaning:** Duty

**Lore:** The fascinating lore of these water birds can be traced to the *Physiologus*, an educational Christian text compiled in the third century by an unknown Greek author. It states that pelicans kill their young in frustration, then revive them in their remorse using their own blood, an allegory for the resurrection of Jesus. This was likely a misunderstanding of how pelicans feed their young: they regurgitate food from the red pouch under their bill, pressing the pouch against their chest to empty it completely. The result is a bloody-looking mess.

Medieval Christians modified this understanding, believing that, in her intense devotion, the pelican mother would wound her breast to feed her young with her own blood. Queen Elizabeth I of England even adopted this symbolism; in a famous portrait by Nicholas Hilliard, she wears a pelican pendant on her chest.

# THE PENGUIN

*Spheniscidae*

**Meaning:** Dignity

**Lore:** Penguins, with their distinguished black and white feathers and upright posture, are noted for their friendly demeanor; the birds generally have no fear of humans.

The Maori people call the Fiordland penguin *tawaki*, named for a god who once walked the earth as a human. The people did not realize Tawaki was a god until he threw off his garb and dressed himself in lightning, revealing his true nature to humankind. The feathered crest of the Fiordland penguin does indeed resemble lightning.

# THE PEREGRINE FALCON

*Falco peregrinus*

**Meaning:** Wandering

**Lore:** The word peregrine, from the Latin *peregrinus,* means "wanderer" or "traveler," and the peregrine falcon—also called simply the peregrine—is associated with a number of deities who undertook sacred journeys. The Norse goddess Freyja was said to wear a cloak of falcon feathers as she traveled between worlds. The ancient Egyptian gods Khonsu and Horus are both depicted as falcon-headed men: Khonsu, whose name also means "traveler" or "wanderer," was the god of the moon, perceived to travel across the sky each night. Similarly, the sky god Horus was thought to contain both the sun and the moon; as he traversed the sky in his falcon form, so too would the sun—his right eye—and the moon, his left.

**See also:** *The Hawk (page 72)*

# THE PETREL

*Procellariiformes*

**Meaning:** A coming storm

**Lore:** Named for Saint Peter, these birds fly close to the water's surface as they look for food, appearing to walk on water as Peter did, briefly, in the Gospel of Matthew.

Eighteenth-century British sailors believed petrels to be harbingers of storms, calling them "Mother Carey's chickens." Related to the mythic Davy Jones, Mother Carey was a supernatural embodiment of the cruelty of the sea.

# THE PHEASANT

*Phasianidae*

**Meaning:** Peace

**Lore:** Like peacocks, male pheasants are more brightly colored than their female counterparts. In China, the golden pheasant is one of the inspirations behind the fèng huang, a mythical bird similar to the phoenix. It appears in both ancient and modern Chinese jewelry, wedding decorations, home decor, and artwork. An immortal bird, it is associated with peace and prosperity.

# THE PHOEBE

*Sayornis*

**Meaning:** Brilliance

**Lore:** The phoebe is a small, gray-colored flycatcher named for the sound of its call ("fee-bee"). Taking the Greek spelling, the name also recalls Phoebe, the mythic Titaness who was the daughter of Uranus and Gaia—the Sky and the Earth—and grandmother to Apollo, Artemis, and Hecate. The original owner of the site of the Oracle of Delphi, Phoebe was associated with prophetic insight. Her name, meaning "bright," was later adapted into a forename for Apollo, the sun god, and an alternative name for Artemis, goddess of the moon.

**See also:** *The Quail (page 150)*

# THE PIGEON

*Columba livia*

**Meaning:** Correspondence

**Lore:** Pigeons were domesticated about five thousand years ago and have a unique homing ability, meaning they instinctively return to their nests even after traveling long distances away. For this reason, they were relied upon to deliver messages in ancient Egypt and by the Mongol emperor Genghis Khan. More recently, they have carried postal messages and wartime communications.

One homing pigeon, Cher Ami, was wounded in battle during the First World War and received honors for managing to deliver a message despite his injuries. During the Second World War, Paddy, an Irish carrier pigeon, received the Dickin Medal for being the first pigeon to arrive in England with news of the successful D-Day invasion. The heroic bird flew over 230 miles across the English Channel in just under five hours.

# THE PLOVER

*Charadriidae*

**Meaning:** Respite

**Lore:** Sometimes mistaken for lapwings, plovers are wading birds found around the world. The golden plover in particular holds a special place in the folklore of Iceland. In this far-northern country, the sight of the first golden plover indicates the arrival of spring. The bird's melancholic calls are said to sing away the snow, reminding Icelanders that the respite of warmer days is ahead.

**See also:** *The Lapwing (page 94)*

# THE POTOO

*Nyctibiidae*

**Meaning:** Longing

**Lore:** The potoo is a fascinating nocturnal bird with cryptic plumage that allows it to blend in with stumps and branches. Native to Central and South America, this elusive bird with large, dark eyes has a ghostly quality. The Shuar people of Ecuador and Peru believe that the moon comes out when it hears the haunting cry of the potoo. According to legend, a man angry with his wife fled to the sky and became the moon; his wife became the potoo, grieving for him at night.

# THE PRAIRIE CHICKEN

*Tympanuchus*

**Meaning:** Rhythm

**Lore:** The prairie chicken is a type of grouse found across the North American prairies. Its scientific name, *Tympanuchus*, comes from the Greek for "holding a drum" and refers to the bird's neck sack, which helps produce its booming call. Both the Blackfoot and Cree peoples have honored the bird for centuries by performing the Prairie Chicken Dance, imitating the beautiful, elaborate mating dance of the male prairie chicken.

# THE PUFFIN

*Fratercula*

**Meaning:** Piety

**Lore:** A black-and-white seabird with a vibrant orange bill, the stocky puffin is a striking sight to behold on rocky coastal cliffs. Its scientific name, *Fratercula*, comes from the Latin *fraterculus*, meaning "little brother," likely because the bird's plumage resembles the robe of a monk. In Ireland, where some believe these sacred birds bear the reincarnated souls of dead friars, the modest, hardworking puffin can be found fishing in turbulent seas or walking with a bowed head along a craggy shore.

# THE QUAIL

*Phasianoidea*

**Meaning:** Refuge

**Lore:** Ground-nesting birds more likely to be heard than seen, quails are often hunted and eaten as game. In Greek mythology, Asteria, the Titaness and daughter of Phoebe, avoided Zeus's advances by turning herself into a quail and diving into the sea, where she became the island of Delos. When Asteria's sister, Leto, was impregnated by Zeus, she avoided Hera's jealous rage by taking refuge on Delos, where she gave birth to her twins, Artemis and Apollo.

**See also:** *The Phoebe (page 138)*

# THE QUETZAL

*Trogonidae*

**Meaning:** Goodness

**Lore:** A small bird with emerald-green feathers, the tropical quetzal is found in the forests of Central and South America. Revered by the Aztecs and Maya, the quetzal was associated with the feathered serpent god, Quetzalcóatl, and symbolized goodness, light, wealth, and freedom. Although rulers and other nobles traditionally wore the feathers of the quetzal, they were careful not to harm the sacred bird while harvesting its plumes. Killing the quetzal was an offense punishable by death.

# THE RAVEN

*Corvus*

**Meaning:** Intelligence

**Lore:** With jet-black feathers and a massive wingspan, the raven's imposing size, keen intelligence, and dark coloring set it apart from all other birds.

In Norse mythology, two ravens called Huginn and Muninn sit atop the shoulders of the one-eyed god Odin. His companions and his spies, the birds fly around the world each day and report back to their master, whispering their findings in his ear.

The raven's association with Odin, considered the father of the Norse gods, suggests an immense respect for the bird's wisdom, but it also acknowledges its role as a scavenger. Like Odin, the god of war, the raven could be ruthless, circling over battlefields scavenging for prey.

**See also:** *The Crow (page 40), The Magpie (page 104)*

# THE RHEA

*Rhea*

**Meaning:** Stability

**Lore:** Distant relative of the ostrich and emu, this large flightless bird is named for the ancient Greek Titaness Rhea, mother of Zeus, Hera, Poseidon, Hestia, Demeter, and Hades. "Rhea" may derive from the Greek *éra*, meaning "ground" or "earth," a suitable name for a land-bound bird.

**See also:** *The Emu (page 54), The Ostrich (page 118)*

# THE ROADRUNNER

*Geococcyx*

**Meaning:** Confusion

**Lore:** The roadrunner, also called the chaparral, is a fast-running bird capable of accelerating up to twenty-six miles per hour. Like the cartoon character of the same name, the bird is notoriously difficult to catch. Apart from its speed, its unique toe anatomy creates X-shaped footprints that could lead in any direction. For this reason, the Pueblo people of the American Southwest re-create the roadrunner's footprints outside the tents of their deceased, hoping to confuse evil spirits and prevent them from following the souls of the dead.

# THE ROOSTER

*Gallus gallus domesticus*

**Meaning:** Betrayal

**Lore:** An adult male chicken is larger than the female of the species, with more brightly colored feathers and a larger red comb atop his head. Known to crow in anticipation of the dawn, the rooster and his call have come to signify daybreak.

Though his sunrise greeting lends the rooster a mostly cheerful reputation, the bird is also associated with betrayal. All four canonical Gospels tell of Jesus' prediction at the Last Supper that his disciple Peter would betray him three times "before the rooster crows." Indeed, Peter did deny Jesus in the lead-up to his crucifixion. In the ninth century, Pope Nicholas I decreed that a rooster be placed atop every church in Europe as a reminder of this betrayal. Because weather vanes were already present on many church steeples, roosters were added to the devices, creating the now ubiquitous "weathercock." The oldest surviving weathercock, the Gallo di Ramperto, was installed around the year 820 atop the bell tower of a church in Brescia, Italy.

# THE SHRIKE

*Laniidae*

**Meaning:** Brutality

**Lore:** Shrikes are notoriously brutal predators, impaling their
victims on sharp sticks, barbed wire, and thorns. Often called
butcherbirds, they ensnare large insects, like crickets and
grasshoppers, as well as mice, lizards, frogs, and even small birds.
Despite their small stature—only about nine inches—they manage
to hunt like much larger raptors. Old folk names for the shrike,
such as *wariangle* or *würgengel,* translate to "choking angel" and hint
at the bird's deceptively sweet appearance.

# THE SNIPE

*Scolopacidae*

**Meaning:** Stubbornness

**Lore:** Snipes, which share a family with curlews and sandpipers, are coastal waders with notably narrow bills. According to an old Chinese proverb, "in the fight between the snipe and the clam, the fisherman has the best of it." In the fable, a snipe pecked at an open clam, which in turn closed its shell on the bird's bill. Neither party would yield, so a passing fisherman netted them both and had them for dinner.

# THE SPARROW

*Passeridae*

**Meaning:** Lust

**Lore:** Petite birds that thrive in both urban and rural habitats, sparrows tend to be associated with sexuality. In ancient Greece, the sparrow was a symbol of Aphrodite, goddess of love. Over the centuries, however, its image became more lustful than loving. In *The Canterbury Tales,* Chaucer described the sparrow as "hot" and "lecherous." At that time in Britain, sparrow pie—believed to be an aphrodisiac—was a common dish. Because the birds were so populous, they were easily captured from the eaves of houses using specially made "sparrow pots."

**See also:** *The Junco (page 84)*

# THE STARLING

*Sturnidae*

**Meaning:** Mimicry

**Lore:** A gifted mimic, the starling gets its name from the way its wings make it look like a star overhead.

A starling appears in the *Mabinogion,* an ancient collection of Welsh folklore, in the story of siblings Branwen and Brân. Branwen, sister of the king of Britain, marries Matholwch, the king of Ireland, and is taken from Wales to live in his country. She is treated cruelly by her new husband but manages to tame a starling and teach it to speak and sends the bird across the sea to her brother Brân to tell him of her strife. When he receives the message, Brân brings his army from Wales to rescue his sister.

While the Welsh myth may seem far-fetched, a historical starling was the beloved pet of Wolfgang Amadeus Mozart. Reportedly, the bird could sing part of Mozart's Piano Concerto no. 17 in G Major. When the starling died just three years after its adoption, the famous composer held an elaborate funeral for his cherished companion and muse.

# THE STONECHAT

*Saxicola*

**Meaning:** Corruption

**Lore:** The stonechat's call sounds a bit like two pebbles knocking against one another, hence the name "stonechat." Scottish folklore claims that the stonechat is the devil's bird, often "chatting" with Satan himself. Another Scottish tale suggests that toads help incubate the eggs of the stonechat. Both creatures were seen as strange and were associated with ill omens.

# THE STORK

*Ciconiidae*

**Meaning:** Family

**Lore:** Large, long-legged wading birds, storks are commonly associated with the arrival of new babies. The origins of this folklore are unclear, but versions of the myth appear across Europe, the Americas, and the Middle East. In Slavic mythology, storks carried unborn souls from Iriy, an otherworldly paradise, to Earth in the springtime.

The bird's association with family may date to the *Lex Ciconaria,* or stork law, of ancient Rome, which required citizens to care for their elderly parents. The law's name drew on a belief among Romans that storks took great care of their families, particularly their elders. Younger storks were even thought to carry their parents on their backs when they became too feeble to fly.

# THE SWALLOW

*Hirundinidae*

**Meaning:** A safe return

**Lore:** The swallow family consists of agile and attractive birds found around the world. Prior to the nineteenth century, European scholars obsessed over where these birds went in the winter. Aristotle suggested that some hibernated; the sixteenth-century Swedish cartographer Olaus Magnus believed they wintered in the mud underwater; and, most outlandishly, the English minister and professor Charles Morton claimed they voyaged to the moon. Eventually, it was discovered that the birds flew as far as South Africa.

Perhaps due to Magnus's theory, sailors began to associate swallows with a safe return. Since the birds were often sighted close to land, spotting one at sea meant the shore was near. Sailor tattoos dating back to the sixteenth century often featured swallows. A swallow on one side of the chest indicated that a sailor had traveled five thousand nautical miles; a second swallow on the opposite side meant he'd sailed twice as far.

**See also:** *The Swift (page 178)*

174

# THE SWAN

*Cygnus*

**Meaning:** Metamorphosis

**Lore:** Elegant, alluring white birds, swans have inspired a number of myths, many of which describe swans that transform into humans, or humans who become swans. In one such tale from Ireland called the "Children of Lir," a jealous stepmother turned her four stepchildren into swans. They lived for nine hundred years and were revered for their enchanting songs and poems.

Perhaps most famous of all swan tales is Tchaikovsky's *Swan Lake*. The ballet features Odette, a princess transformed into the titular bird by an evil sorcerer, Baron von Rothbart. Odette can only take a human form between midnight and daybreak, which is when Prince Siegfried falls in love with her. The sorcerer tricks Siegfried into professing his love, not for Odette but for Rothbart's daughter, Odile. When Siegfried realizes his mistake, he finds Odette, who is cursed to remain a swan forever. The two throw themselves into the lake, and their love breaks the curse.

**See also:** *The Duck (page 48)*

176

# THE SWIFT

*Apodidae*

**Meaning:** Restlessness

**Lore:** The swift is associated with constant motion. Commonly confused for swallows, some swifts can spend up to ten months flying nonstop. Because the bird's short legs are adapted for clinging to vertical surfaces, like trees or chimneys, it is rarely seen landing on the ground. It was even once thought to be footless, a quality reflected in its scientific name, *apus,* from the Greek for "without feet."

The swift is believed to be the inspiration behind the heraldic symbol of the martlet, which often represented a fourth son. Due to the law of primogeniture, which originated in medieval Europe and lasted into the twentieth century, fourth sons had no land inheritance and were seen as wanderers—much like the restless swift.

**See also:** *The Swallow (page 174)*

# THE THRASHER

*Toxostoma*

**Meaning:** Harmony

**Lore:** Named for the noisy way it thrashes about on the ground foraging for food, the thrasher is a noted vocalist and close relative of the catbird and mockingbird. An individual thrasher knows between one thousand and three thousand song phrases, the largest documented repertoire of any bird. Due to its two-sided syrinx, or vocal organ, this bird can sing two harmonious tones at once, producing a truly unique sound.

**See also:** *The Catbird (page 28), The Mockingbird (page 106)*

# THE THRUSH

*Turdidae*

**Meaning:** To be heard but not seen

**Lore:** Known for its ethereal song, the thrush plays an important role in a legend told by the Oneida people of North America: Long ago, as the Creator walked through the forests, he realized that birds made no sound. To remedy this, he held a competition to award the birds with individual songs. Each bird would fly as far as it could into the sky, and when it could fly no farther, it would find its song. The bird who flew the farthest would receive the most beautiful song of all. Desiring to win the competition, the thrush hid himself on the back of the eagle, who he was sure would fly the farthest. Once the eagle had flown as far as he could go, the thrush took off, flying even farther into the sky. There, he heard a beautiful song, which he learned to sing before flying back to the earth. When he returned, the other birds were displeased with him, and the thrush felt ashamed of his actions. He chose to hide away in the woods, where he is rarely seen, but he can still be heard singing his enchanting song.

# THE TITMOUSE

*Baeolophus*

**Meaning:** Dishonesty

**Lore:** Small and noisy, titmice are closely related to chickadees and play a role in the Cherokee legend of Spearfinger, in which an honest chickadee helps the villagers vanquish an evil witch. Before the chickadee can help, the arrogant titmouse misleads the villagers by telling them to aim their arrows at the witch's heart. But the arrows they shoot bounce off Spearfinger's chest and are broken. Revealed to be a liar, the titmouse is captured, and its tongue is cut off as punishment.

**See also:** *The Chickadee (page 30)*

# THE TOUCAN

*Ramphastidae*

**Meaning:** First impressions

**Lore:** Magnificent birds with contrasting plumage and brightly colored bills, toucans are revered by Indigenous peoples in Central and South America, where their feathers often feature in ceremonial headdresses.

Myths about the toucan frequently focus on its beak, which, in addition to being vibrant, is one-third the length of the bird's body. A Brazilian folktale claims that the toucan became king of the birds by perching inside a hole in a tree, displaying his bill but hiding his body. The other birds accepted him as king, believing such an impressive beak could only belong to a massive bird. When the king finally emerged from his hole, however, he was mocked for his unusual proportions.

# THE TURKEY

*Meleagris*

**Meaning:** Nourishment

**Lore:** In the United States, the turkey is primarily a symbol of the Thanksgiving holiday, associated with hearty nourishment. However, long before the American holiday developed, these birds were revered by the ancient Maya. The bones of the domestic turkey have been found at the Jaguar Paw Temple in modern-day Guatemala, far from the bird's natural habitat, indicating it was transported across long distances, likely for rituals and ceremonies. Images of the turkey native to Central America, the ocellated turkey, once decorated Maya temple walls and manuscripts. It was also eaten by the upper classes and by religious leaders.

An Apache legend describes the turkey as a bird of nourishment, but not in the form of meat. In the folktale, a turkey shakes his wings and produces four types of corn seeds, which are then planted, providing ample food for the community.

# THE VULTURE

*Accipitriformes*

**Meaning:** Rebirth

**Lore:** As scavenger birds, vultures feed on carrion, the decaying flesh of animals. Because of this, we tend to associate them with death. In ancient Egypt, however, these birds were revered as symbols of rebirth. The goddess Nekhbet was depicted as a vulture, and ancient Egyptians believed all vultures were female, born from eggs without the need of male involvement. Thus, the birds were linked to motherhood, and they turned death into life by feeding on animal remains: a circle of life, death, and rebirth. The wives of pharaohs, female pharaohs, and high-ranking priestesses all wore vulture crowns to honor Nekhbet and invoke her protection.

# THE WARBLER

*Emberizoidea, Sylvioidea*

**Meaning:** Embellishment

**Lore:** Two distinct families of warblers come from the Eastern and Western Hemispheres (Sylvioidea are found in Eurasia and Africa, and Emberizoidea are found in the Americas), and while the two groups are not closely related, their songs are similar. Warblers are distinguished by their trilling calls, and therefore we call singers—especially those who tend to embellish—warblers.

The Japanese bush warbler, known in Japan as *uguisu*, is especially appreciated for its expressive song. Typically coinciding with the blooming of plum blossoms in February, the warbler's mating call heralds the coming spring.

# THE WAXWING

*Bombycilla*

**Meaning:** Malady

**Lore:** Named for the red markings on their wingtips said to resemble drops of sealing wax, these birds became associated with illness during the Middle Ages. Due to their migratory wanderings during cold winters, their sudden arrival in large flocks often coincided with outbreaks of the bubonic plague in parts of western Europe. While in reality waxwings aren't especially likely to carry or spread disease, the association stuck. To this day, the Dutch call the waxwing *pestvogel*, meaning "plague bird."

# THE WEAVERBIRD

*Ploceidae*

**Meaning:** Creativity

**Lore:** Weaverbirds are named for their elaborate nests, woven from leaves, reeds, grasses, and twigs. The birds' nest designs vary greatly among species. Some weaverbirds, aptly called "sociable weavers," create apartment-like nests with individual entrances for different mating pairs. Others build multiple nests in a single tree, and still others build solitary nests. The male weaverbird is the architect, and when his masterpiece is finished, he invites a potential mate to his palace. If the female approves, she mates with him; if she is not impressed, the male bird may try again, constructing another nest.

# THE WOODPECKER

*Picidae*

**Meaning:** Toughness

**Lore:** Both male and female woodpeckers are known for drumming their beaks against hollow logs, dead trees, and even metal, creating a loud, reverberating noise that attracts a mate and declares their territory. Adapted to this behavior, the skull of the woodpecker is spongy, and its long tongue wraps around the brain to protect it. Likewise, the bird's tough neck muscles and stiff beak absorb repetitive blows, preventing head injury.

In Norse mythology, the woodpecker is sacred to Thor, the god of thunder and lightning. Like Thor, the woodpecker wields his "hammer," producing a sound that some liken to rolling thunder.

# THE WREN

*Troglodytidae*

**Meaning:** Restoration

**Lore:** Little birds with loud voices, wrens are closely associated with *Lá an Dreoilín,* or Wren Day, on December 26. This Irish celebration traditionally involved hunting a wren, placing its body atop a decorated pole, and parading it through the village. Today, there is no hunt, and a stuffed wren is used in place of the live bird, but "mummers," "straw boys," or "wren boys" still dress in elaborate straw costumes to perform the ritual. Wren Day has been revived in parts of the United Kingdom, and similar traditions also have been observed in Spain and France. While the exact origins of this tradition are unknown, it is likely related to the winter solstice: the robin, associated with warmth, defeats the wren, a bird of winter, restoring the sun for the new year.

**See also:** *The European Robin (page 56)*

# ACKNOWLEDGMENTS

Writing and illustrating a second book is no easy task, and the people below know this all too well. Thank you for putting up with me.

Thank you to my husband and my very best friend, Nick, for reading everything I write, being excited about the birds, and taking care of me, Molly, and the garden. You inspire me every day.

Thank you to my family, especially Mom and Dad, Liana, Hannah, and Felix. I wouldn't be here without your love and patience.

Thank you to my editor, Melissa, for always knowing what I want to say and helping me say it better. I have been supremely lucky to work with you for many years, and hopefully for many years to come. A very big thank-you to everyone at Andrews McMeel.

Thank you to my agent, Alyssa, for your limitless help, guidance, and knowledge. I truly do not know what I would do without you.

Thank you to Molly for your endless love and especially for all the nosy nudges that tell me to stop working and take you on a walk.

Thank you to my friends, especially Ginnie, Libby, Dani, Jen, Brad, Kayla, Jeriann, and Andrew. I am a lucky duck to count you among my inner circle.

And most of all, thank you to the birds. While working on this book, I kept seeing specific birds on the same day I was illustrating them. Was this a form of magic or just the frequency illusion? I prefer to think of it as magic, especially when my heron friend appeared after many weeks away, beak tucked beneath its wing, standing alone in the shallow creek. From my chickadees to my crows, my hawks to my vultures, my cardinals to my woodpeckers, seeing you brings me joy. I hope you like the birdseed and the plants.

# INDEX

*By Meaning*

## ENCOURAGEMENT

The American Robin . . . Hope

The Bluebird . . . Patience; Hope

The California Condor . . . A new beginning

The Cardinal . . . Confidence

The Cassowary . . . Defying expectations

The Catbird . . . Advantage

The Coot . . . Tenacity

The Cormorant . . . Good luck; Victory

The Cowbird . . . Stealth

The Crane . . . Fortune

The Dove . . . Love; Hope

The Eagle . . . Strength; Focus

The Flamingo . . . Survival

The Heron . . . A positive message

The Hummingbird . . . Might

The Lark . . . Levity

The Little Owl . . . Wisdom

The Loon . . . A helping hand

The Lyrebird . . . Mentorship

The Osprey . . . Ferocity

The Ostrich . . . Strength

The Parrot . . . Bravery

The Pheasant . . . Peace

The Phoebe . . . Brilliance

The Plover . . . Respite

The Quail . . . Refuge

The Quetzal . . . Goodness

The Raven . . . Intelligence

The Rhea . . . Stability

The Toucan . . . First impressions

The Vulture . . . Rebirth

The Warbler . . . Embellishment

The Woodpecker . . . Toughness

The Wren . . . Restoration

## FAITH AND SPIRITUALITY

The Cormorant . . . Good luck; Victory

The Dove . . . Love; Hope

The Flamingo . . . Survival

The Gull . . . Duality

The Jacana . . . A miracle

The Kingfisher . . . Devotion

The Owl . . . An ill omen

The Peacock . . . Reverence

The Pelican . . . Duty

The Pheasant . . . Peace

The Puffin . . . Piety

## GRATITUDE

The Gannet . . . A gift

The Goose . . . Wealth

The Kookaburra . . . Joy

The Pigeon . . . Correspondence

The Plover . . . Respite

The Quail . . . Refuge

The Turkey . . . Nourishment

## GRIEF AND SYMPATHY

The Dodo . . . Obsolescence

The European Robin . . . Compassion

The Kite . . . Mourning

The Magpie . . . Prophecy

The Nightingale . . . Unrequited love

The Owl . . . An ill omen

The Potoo . . . Longing

The Roadrunner . . . Confusion

The Shrike . . . Brutality

The Waxwing . . . Malady

The Wren . . . Restoration

## HEARTBREAK

The Catbird . . . Advantage

The Cuckoo . . . Duplicity

The Harpy Eagle . . . Cruelty

The Hornbill . . . Consolation

The Junco . . . Winter

The Kite . . . Mourning

The Kiwi . . . Sacrifice

The Lapwing . . . Deceit

The Magpie . . . Prophecy

The Nightingale . . . Unrequited love

The Owl . . . An ill omen

The Potoo . . . Longing

The Roadrunner . . . Confusion

The Rooster . . . Betrayal

The Shrike . . . Brutality

The Stonechat . . . Corruption

The Titmouse . . . Dishonesty

The Waxwing . . . Malady

The Wren . . . Restoration

## LOVE AND RELATIONSHIPS

The Chickadee . . . Honesty

The Dove . . . Love; Hope

The Egret . . . Rare beauty

The European Robin . . . Compassion

The Finch . . . Domesticity

The Kingfisher . . . Devotion

The Kookaburra . . . Joy

The Lyrebird . . . Mentorship

The Magpie . . . Prophecy

The Parakeet . . . Reunion

The Potoo . . . Longing

The Quail . . . Refuge

The Quetzal . . . Goodness

The Sparrow . . . Lust

The Stork . . . Family

## TRAVEL

The Arctic Tern . . . Travels

The Booby . . . Curiosity

The Emu . . . Celestial guidance

The Junco . . . Winter

The Parakeet . . . Reunion

The Peregrine Falcon . . . Wandering

The Petrel . . . A coming storm

The Quail . . . Refuge

The Rhea . . . Stability

The Swallow . . . A safe return

The Swift . . . Restlessness

## WARNING AND DISPLEASURE

The Bittern . . . Fear of the unknown

The Booby . . . Curiosity

The Canary . . . A warning

The Cowbird . . . Stealth

The Cuckoo . . . Duplicity

The Grackle . . . Intrusion

The Harpy Eagle . . . Cruelty

The Hawk . . . Intensity

The Lapwing . . . Deceit

The Magpie . . . Prophecy

The Nightjar . . . A false accusation

The Osprey . . . Ferocity

The Owl . . . An ill omen

The Petrel . . . A coming storm

The Rooster . . . Betrayal

The Shrike . . . Brutality

The Snipe . . . Stubbornness

The Stonechat . . . Corruption

The Titmouse . . . Dishonesty

The Waxwing . . . Malady

## WELL-WISHES AND CONGRATULATIONS

The California Condor . . . A new beginning

The Cassowary . . . Defying expectations

The Cormorant . . . Good luck; Victory

The Crow . . . Cleverness

The Flamingo . . . Survival

The Gannet . . . A gift

The Goose . . . Wealth

The Parrot . . . Bravery

The Pigeon . . . Correspondence

The Plover . . . Respite

The Vulture . . . Rebirth

# ABOUT THE AUTHOR

**Jessica Roux** is a Nashville-based illustrator and
plant and animal enthusiast. She loves exploring
in her own backyard and being surrounded by an
abundance of nature. Using subdued colors and
rhythmic shapes, she renders flora and fauna in
intricate detail reminiscent of old-world beauty.

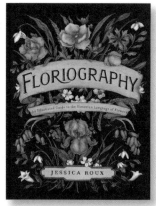